NATIONAL GEOGRAPHIC

T0308162

Our Human Footprint

PATHFINDER EDITION

By Barbara H. Seeber

CONTENTS

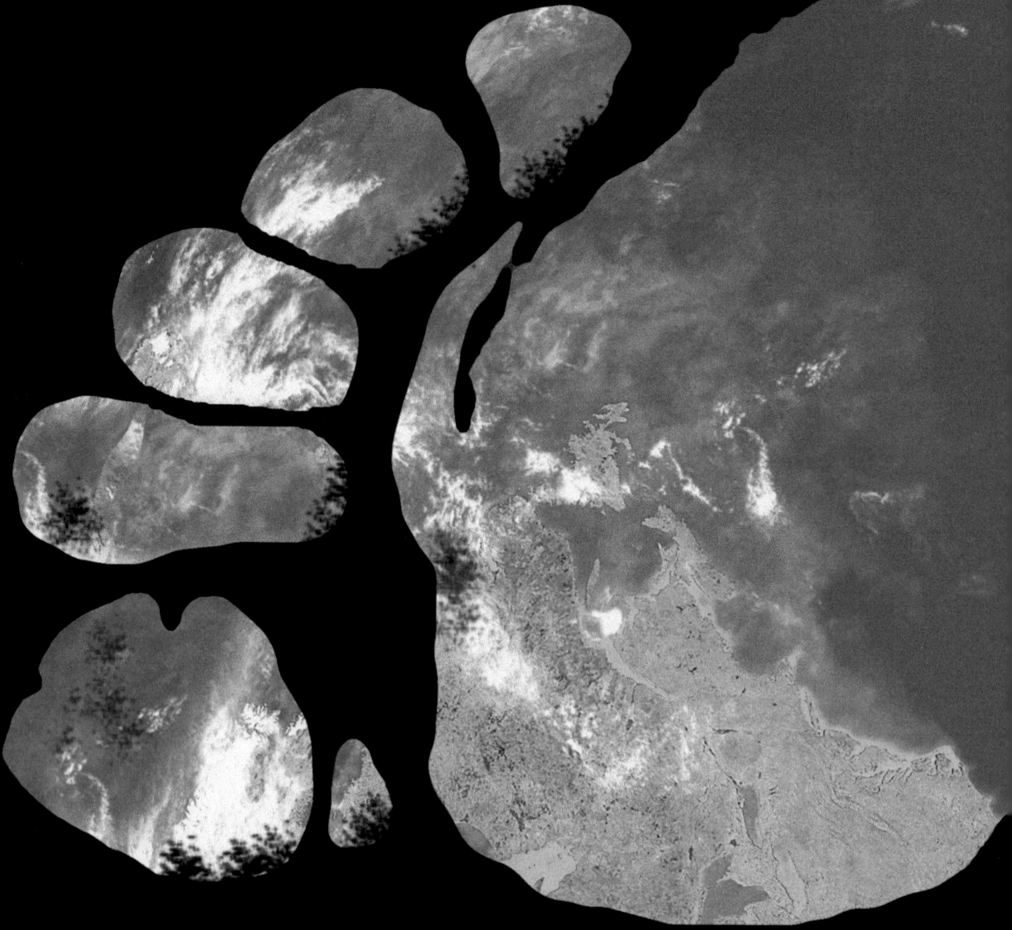

Our Huma

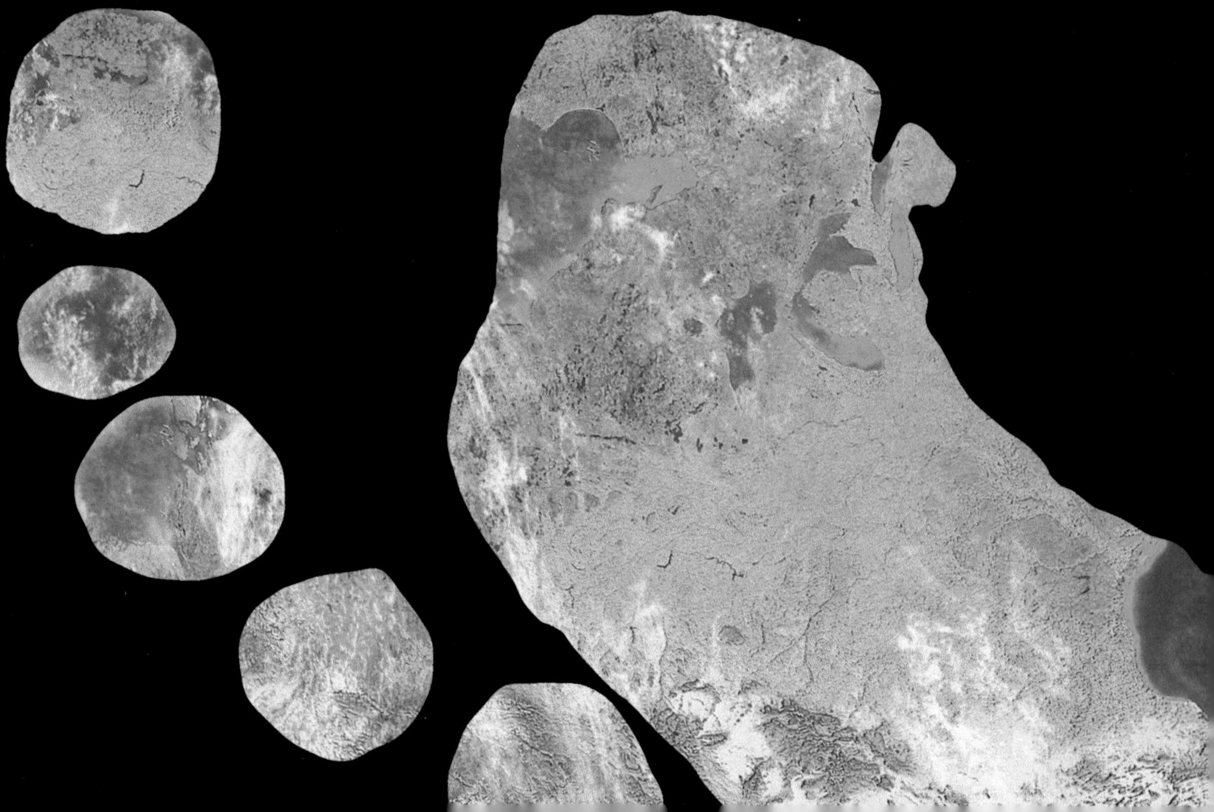

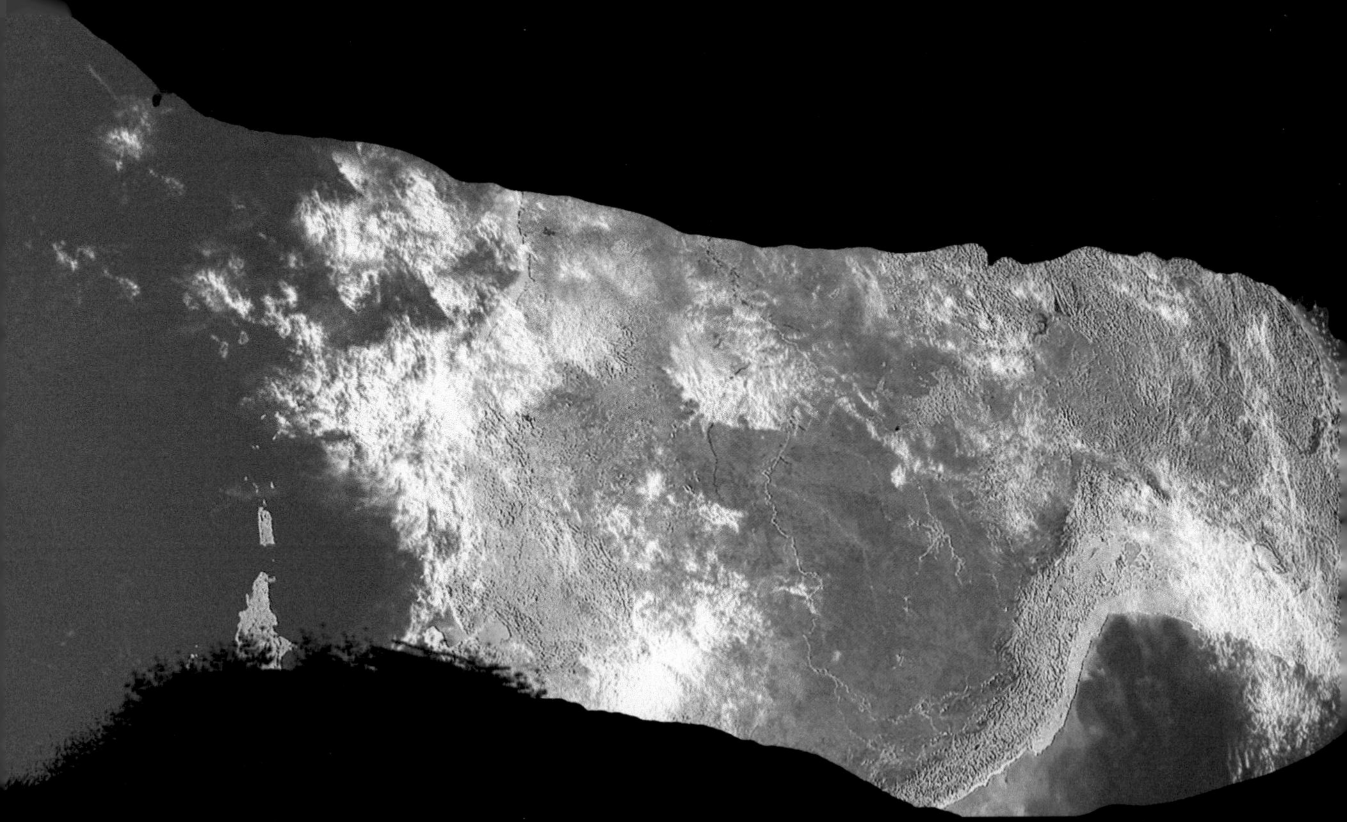

Footprint

How large an impact does one individual have on the planet? The author decided to find out. She discovered that all those must-have T-shirts, burgers, and long showers really start to add up.

By Barbara H. Seeber

The average person in the U.S. consumes a lot in a lifetime. Take a look below to see some of it.

I'm not a litterbug, *and I don't trash the planet. In fact, I think going green is great, but the truth is I had no idea how the things I do all add up.*

I'm talking about my human footprint—that's all the stuff I buy, use, or throw away. Everything I do affects Earth's health. That's both good news and bad news.

Trash Travels

Here's the bad part. On average, each person in the United States throws out more than two kilograms (almost five pounds) of trash every single day!

Most gets buried underground in smelly **landfills**, and it stays there until it decays. Some things take hundreds, or even thousands, of years to completely **decompose**.

Some trash goes into incinerators, or ovens, that burn up the trash. In the process, we send smoke and chemicals into the air.

Bits of litter also wash down storm drains, and they end up in our rivers and oceans. Hikers even leave trash behind when they climb mountains. Mount Everest is the highest mountain in the world—it is also the highest trash dump!

Trash is just one part of the picture. Earth's natural resources are another part. We **consume** a lot of them. We use oil to produce gasoline and plastic. We mine coal for energy and aluminum for cans. We draw water for growing crops and taking showers. Americans make up 5 percent of the world's population; yet of all the energy used in the entire world, Americans gobble up 26 percent.

Hot Air

A person's **carbon footprint** also affects Earth. That's how much carbon dioxide (CO_2) one person **releases**, or sends, into the atmosphere. I'm not talking about the little bit of air we breathe out. I'm talking about the large amounts of CO_2 we make by using energy.

We mainly make CO_2 by burning coal, oil, or gas, and we use these fuels to do everything from driving our cars to lighting up our houses. Each American family sends about 68 kilograms (150 pounds) of CO_2 into the air every day.

Keeping Track

This may sound grim, but there is good news, too. I can do something about it! I don't have to throw away so much trash. I can use fewer resources and less energy. I don't have to be a Bigfoot. I can shrink my footprint.

First, I have to figure out just how big my footprint is. I'll keep track of my daily habits, or the usual way I do things, and see how they relate to trash, energy, and natural resources. What do I do every day? How much of an impact do my choices have on the planet? I have a feeling I'm in for some surprises!

Take Out the Trash. *People in the U.S. produce so much trash, they export, or send, it to other countries.*

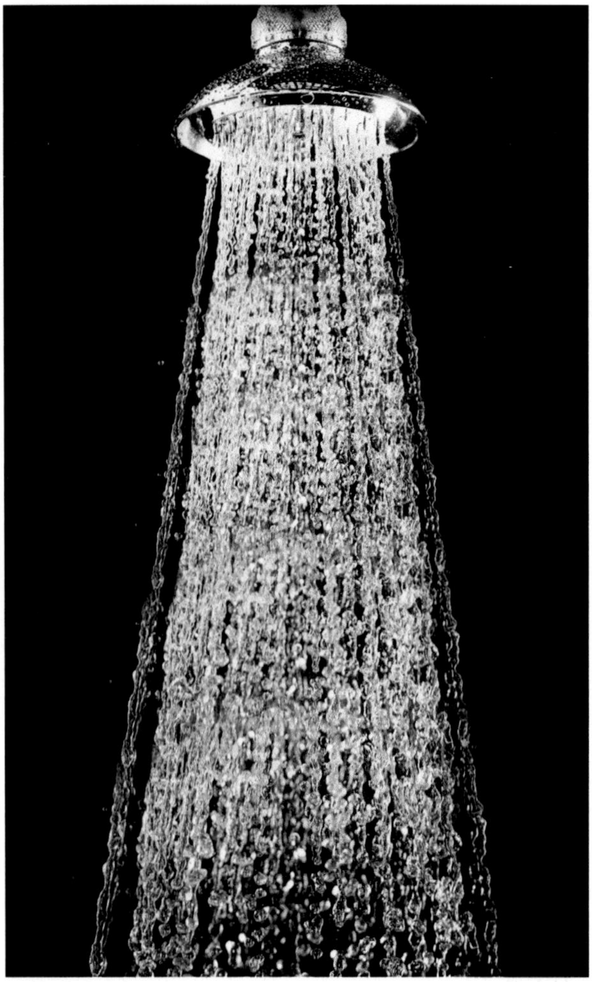

Down the Drain. *In the U.S., one person uses about 380 liters (100 gallons) of water each day.*

Carry Out Trash. *Americans eat lots of fast food and other convenience food. The bags, boxes, and wrappers pile up in landfills.*

Early Start

Every day as soon as I wake up, I check my email. Oh no! I left the computer on all night. That wastes energy.

The computer uses energy even when it's turned off. That's called vampire power, but there's a way to stop it. Unplug the computer. In fact, many appliances secretly suck up energy while plugged in, even when turned off. So I also unplug the chargers for my cell phone and my other electronic stuff.

Next stop: my shower. I love long, hot showers, but today, I take a short, lukewarm shower. It wasn't so bad. The good part is I saved water and energy.

Then I decide to bike to work. The average U.S. car pumps about a pound of CO_2 into the air per mile. Using my own energy is a plus for me and the planet.

Lunch Lessons

At noon, I take my lunch out of a reusable container. That's a change. Last week, I packed my sandwich in a plastic bag. Afterwards, I tossed the bag and my plastic water bottle. Sure, I didn't litter, but creating this trash wasn't so great either. Why?

It takes 12 million gallons of oil to make a year's worth of the plastic bags used in the U.S. That's a lot of natural resources. Plus, Americans throw away 100 billion plastic bags a year. Many end up in landfills. So do the plastic bottles. Although many people regularly **recycle** bottles, most people still don't. So most plastic bottles end up in landfills, too. They take a thousand years to decompose. On top off all that, plastic factories use a lot of energy and make a lot of CO_2. Well, that was last week. This week, I'm still in the game.

Need or Want?

Later, I ride my bike to the mall. Look at that cute orange T-shirt! I want it, but it takes cotton, chemicals, and hundreds of gallons of water to make one shirt. Plus, this one traveled thousands of miles from China. Sigh. I think I'll wait until I really need new clothes.

I also decide against, or choose not to buy, a new cell phone for now. Chemicals in old cell batteries can create problems in landfills. They can seep into soil and water, and that causes pollution. Luckily, cell phones can be recycled. That's what I'll do when I really need to buy a new one.

Now I'm hungry. I grab a quick burger. Yum! Then I get a sinking feeling in my stomach. A paper bag, cup, straw, wrapper, plastic utensils, napkin—the trash adds up.

I also have to think about what goes into making the burger. Cows need food and water. The bread and meat have to be processed, shipped, stored, and cooked. But now I know.

To Buy or Not to Buy? *Buy only what you need. It takes chemicals and hundreds of gallons of water to make one T-shirt.*

Seeing the Light

I head home, but I still have time today to make some good choices. I replace my 60-watt light bulbs with new 15-watt fluorescent ones. These use less energy and last longer.

It's time to tally up my day. I made a few mistakes, but I made good choices, too. I threw away less trash. I used less energy. I know more ways to cut down on my use of Earth's resources. Bit by bit, it all adds up.

I turn out my bedside lamp. My hand accidentally brushes the new bulb, but it's not hot. It only used energy to make light, not heat. Now that's cool! As I fall asleep, I feel happy. I shrunk my footprint today.

Extreme Recycling

No one ever said shrinking my footprint would be easy. Some days, I wonder if the little bits I do can make a difference. Then I remember that I'm not alone.

Around the world, many people are pitching in. Friends of planet Earth are popping up all over the place. Working together, we can have a big impact.

In 2001, some New Jersey college students started a different kind of recycling company. These garbage go-getters looked at the nation's trash and saw a goldmine, or successful way to make money.

They now collect waste from about 20,000 schools. What do they do with ten million drink pouches, 50,000 energy bar wrappers, one million cookie wrappers, and more? Make toys and school supplies!

Cereal boxes become notebooks. Newspapers turn into pencils. Cookie wrappers soar to new heights as kites. I'm glad someone's turning trash into treasure.

Trash People

Turning trash into art is another cool idea. German artist HA Schult makes Trash People. Old cans are the faces. Computers are the torsos. Strings of plastic cups, bottles, and cell phones are shiny, bumpy legs and arms.

Schult has made 1,000 of these life-size figures. He has set them up in places all over the world. They've visited the Egyptian pyramids, the Great Wall of China, and even National Geographic in Washington, D.C. What do you suppose he's telling us?

Trash People. *A clever artist turns trash into sculptures. The Trash People have been displayed all over the world, including near the Swiss Alps.*

Old Is New Again. *People reuse candy wrappers to make bags and recycle glass to make bracelets.*

THINGS YOU CAN DO TO SHRINK YOUR HUMAN FOOTPRINT

1. **Bike, walk, or carpool. A car releases about a pound of CO_2 per mile.**
2. **Don't use the drive-through. A running engine lets out more CO_2 than restarting a car.**
3. **Turn off lights and TVs when you leave the room. The energy needed to watch an hour of TV releases a half-pound of CO_2.**
4. **Take shorter showers. A shower uses about five gallons of water per minute.**
5. **Use reusable bags. Tossed plastic bags can end up in the ocean. Animals might eat them and get sick.**
6. **Buy things with less packaging. About a third of what we throw away is packaging.**
7. **Recycle. Every ton of recycled paper saves 8,000 gallons of water and 17 trees.**
8. **Plant a tree. One tree absorbs about 48 pounds of CO_2 a year.**

Picked Clean

In Sydney, Australia, a factory works overtime. It's not making new products. In fact, it has a dis-assembly line. What is it taking apart? Sydney's trash.

Trucks bring in tons of garbage. Then high-tech equipment goes to work. Robotic arms empty bags of trash. Workers remove lead, mercury, and other toxic, or poisonous, materials. Electric currents push recyclable metals into a bin. Air jets blow paper and plastic into other bins.

What's left goes into a tank. Some becomes a gas. Some turns into compost, or fertilizer. By the end, almost 75 percent of Sydney's trash is recycled. Only 25 percent gets buried in a landfill. That company definitely deserves a high-tech high-five!

WORDWISE

carbon footprint: amount of carbon dioxide a person puts into the atmosphere

consume: use fuel, energy, or resources

decompose: break up

landfill: trash that is buried and covered with dirt

recycle: put things through a process so they can be used again

release: let things go into the atmosphere

HOW BIG Is Your FOOTPRINT?

You change Earth with all the stuff you buy, use, and throw away. This is called your human footprint. How your footprint changes Earth is up to you.

Save Water

We use water to make nearly everything we eat or use. Scientists have found out how much water it takes to make a dollar's worth of some things you use every day. How much water does it take to make a dollar's worth of cotton? It takes 4,291 liters, or 1,300 gallons, of water. What about a dollar's worth of electricity? It takes 1,703 liters. That is 450 gallons of water.

Here's another way to think about it. It takes about 24,000 liters, or 6,334 gallons, of water to grow the food for a cow. That cow will be made into a hamburger that weighs 0.1 kilograms (1/4 pound). And it takes additional water to make the cheese, bun, and ketchup that go with the burger.

Instead of using plastic bags, try a reusable bag. That will save energy and cut down on the amount of trash you make.

Save Energy

By making the right choices, you can have a big impact on our environment. For example, do you use plastic bags? Most people do. Just think of all the ways you can use plastic bags. You might carry groceries in plastic bags. You might put your lunch in plastic bags. You might even put trash in plastic bags. All those plastic bags quickly add up. So do the natural resources used to make them.

People worldwide use a lot of plastic bags. Some scientists estimate that people use between 500 billion and a trillion plastic bags each year. If each of those bags were the size of a plastic grocery bag, they would stretch from Earth to the moon and back again 400 times.

It takes a lot of energy to make plastic bags, too. Did you know that in the United States alone, it takes 12 million gallons of oil to make a year's worth of plastic bags?

Instead of using plastic bags that you end up throwing away, use a reusable bag. That will save resources, like oil, needed to make plastic. It will also save energy and create less trash.

Reduce Waste

You also can buy products that come in less packaging. Less packaging uses less paper and plastic. Most people just throw away the packaging after opening their purchase. You can make sure you recycle the paper and plastic wrapping from anything you buy. Recycling paper not only saves trees, it also saves water. One ton of recycled paper saves 17 trees and 30,283 liters (8,000 gallons) of water.

Caring for our planet may seem like a big job. It is. Yet it can start with small steps. It can start with you. You can decide what to buy, what to recycle, and what to reuse. You can change your human footprint. If everyone makes the right decisions, then we all will be able to live on a sustainable planet.

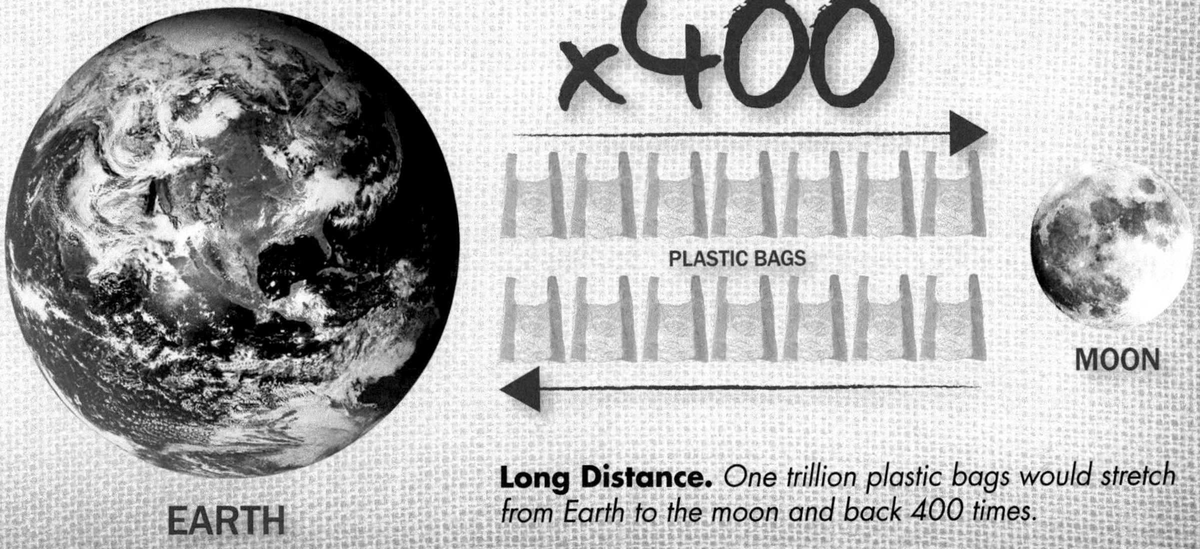

Long Distance. *One trillion plastic bags would stretch from Earth to the moon and back 400 times.*

Reduce, Reuse, Recycle

Shrink your human footprint and answer these questions.

1. Describe the three things that make up a human footprint.
2. What happens to trash after it is thrown away?
3. In your opinion, what are the three best ways to shrink your human footprint? Explain your choices.
4. What are some ways people around the world reuse trash?
5. How does the diagram on page 11 help you understand the quantity of plastic bags used in a year?